D0496911

Muslim

Richard Tames

W

FRANKLIN WATTS

This edition 2004

Franklin Watts
96 Leonard Street
London
EC2A 4XD

Franklin Watts Australia
45–51 Huntley Street
Alexandria
NSW 2015

Series Editor: Sarah Ridley
Designer: Liz Black
Copy Editor: Nicola Barber
Picture Researchers: Brooks Krikler
Illustrators: pages 5 and 20 Aziz Khan; pages 18-
19 Piers Harper
Photographer (activities): Peter Millard
Consultant: Dr M Ahsan and the Islamic
Foundation

Photographs: Eye Ubiquitous 24t; Robert Harding
Picture Library 8t, 8b, 10r, 21; Michael Holford
cover (left), 6b; Hutchison Library 13t, 13b, 14t,
24b, 30; ICOREC/Circa Photo Library, Manchester
Metropolitan University 27b; Panos Pictures 27t,
28; Richard Tames 6t; Trip cover (right), 4t, 4b,
7t, 9t, 9b, 10l, 12, 15tl, 15br, 20, 22t, 22b, 23bl,
23tr, 25t, 29.

With thanks also to the IQRA Trust for their help
with this book.

A CIP catalogue record for this book is available
from the British Library.
Dewey Decimal Classification Number 297

ISBN: 0 7496 5232 2

Printed in Dubai, UAE

CONTENTS

A MAN AND A MESSAGE

Islam is the religion based on the teachings of the Prophet Muhammad, who lived in Arabia about 1,400 years ago. Followers of Islam are called Muslims. Islam is the main religion of the Middle East and North Africa, and of countries such as Pakistan, Bangladesh, Indonesia and Nigeria. However, Muslims have travelled and settled in many countries round the world and formed their own communities.

Pilgrims enter the cave on Mount Hira where Muhammad went to think and pray.

The mosque at Medina where Muhammad is buried.

MUHAMMAD

Muhammad was born in the city of Mecca in around 570CE (CE stands for Common or Christian Era). Although he was orphaned as a boy, Muhammad grew up to become a successful merchant. Muhammad could have had an easy life but he was troubled by the evils he saw around him - greed, cruelty and superstition. Many of the Arabs were pagans who worshipped idols of wood or stone. Some believed that their tribe was protected by a special god of its own.

Muhammad was a thoughtful man, and he often went into the mountains to think and pray. At the age of forty, he received a revelation (divine message) from God to pass on to the people of Mecca about how they ought to live their lives. These revelations continued to come to Muhammad for the rest of his life and became the words of the Qur'an. God directed him to preach the messages of the Qur'an to all people.

MUHAMMAD'S TEACHINGS

Muhammad taught that there was only one God and that it was wrong to worship idols. He told people to be kind and generous to the poor and weak, and not to gamble or drink alcohol.

Muhammad's teachings upset many powerful people in Mecca who did not like to be criticised. They also thought that if Muhammad spoke against the worship of idols, then the idol-worshippers might stay away from Mecca and they would lose trade. So Muhammad and his followers were forced to leave the city and settle at the oasis of Medina. For ten years there was war between the people of Mecca and the Muslims. In the end the Muslims were victorious. Muhammad returned to Mecca in triumph and smashed all the idols in the city's main shrine, the *Ka'ba*.

After Muhammad's death, in 632CE, the Muslims spread Islam from Spain to India, and later into Africa and South-East Asia.

The map shows the percentage of Muslims in the population of each country.

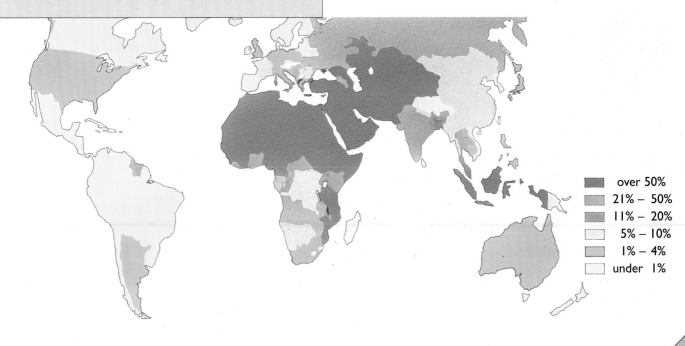

	over 50%
	21% – 50%
	11% – 20%
	5% – 10%
	1% – 4%
	under 1%

THE BELIEFS OF ISLAM

Islam is especially close to two of the other great religions - Judaism and Christianity. All three religions are based on belief in one God and respect for sacred books which record God's teachings. All three command their followers to act with justice and kindness and to show a special care for the poor and weak.

The splendour of sunset proclaims God, the Creator of the world.

Muslims, like Jews, respect Abraham as a prophet and look upon Jerusalem as a holy city. Muslims call Jesus *Isa* and respect him as a true prophet and a great teacher. But, unlike Christians, they do not believe that Jesus is the Son of God or that he died when he was crucified. Instead Muslims believe that God took Jesus up off the cross straight into Heaven.

Muslims believe that God sent many prophets to teach people how to lead good lives from the time of Adam, the first man, onwards. For Muslims, Muhammad was the 'seal of the prophets', the very last one whose words summed up all the important teachings of those who had gone before him.

The Dome on the Rock, Jerusalem, a holy city for Muslims, Jews and Christians.

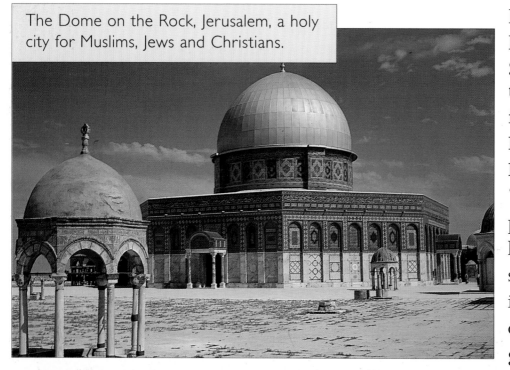

THE FIVE PILLARS OF ISLAM

Many Muslims explain Islam as being like a strong building held up by five pillars. The five pillars represent belief, prayer, alms giving, fasting and pilgrimage.

Muslim men assemble for the Friday noon prayer outside a crowded mosque in Tashkent, Uzbekistan.

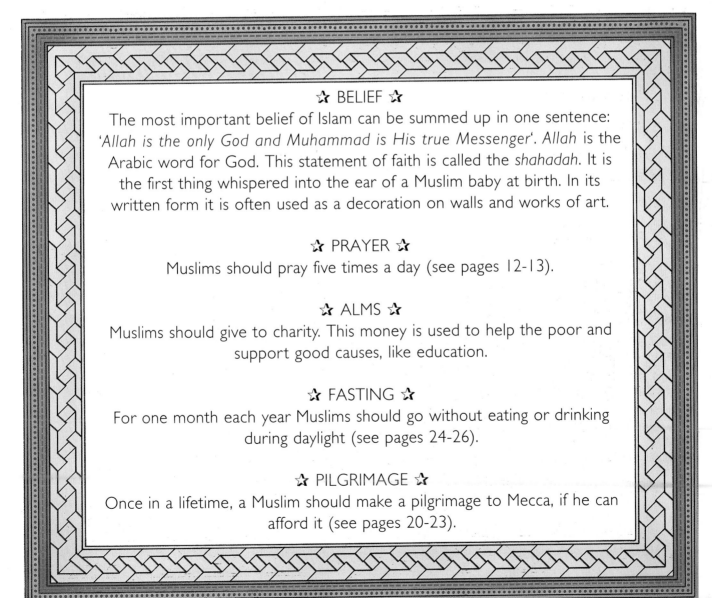

☆ BELIEF ☆
The most important belief of Islam can be summed up in one sentence: *'Allah is the only God and Muhammad is His true Messenger'*. *Allah* is the Arabic word for God. This statement of faith is called the *shahadah*. It is the first thing whispered into the ear of a Muslim baby at birth. In its written form it is often used as a decoration on walls and works of art.

☆ PRAYER ☆
Muslims should pray five times a day (see pages 12-13).

☆ ALMS ☆
Muslims should give to charity. This money is used to help the poor and support good causes, like education.

☆ FASTING ☆
For one month each year Muslims should go without eating or drinking during daylight (see pages 24-26).

☆ PILGRIMAGE ☆
Once in a lifetime, a Muslim should make a pilgrimage to Mecca, if he can afford it (see pages 20-23).

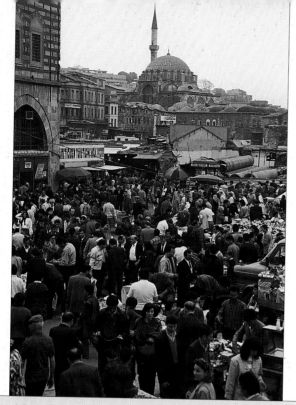

Almost everyone in this street scene in Istanbul, Turkey, is wearing Western dress.

In Riyadh, Saudi Arabia, Western dress is the exception. Most men and women do not mix together outside the home.

ISLAM AND THE LAW

Muslim countries vary in how much Islam affects the government and daily life. In Turkey, even though almost everyone is a Muslim, due to Western influence, the law and religion are kept separate and men and women mix together freely in public places.

In Saudi Arabia the Islamic holy book, the Qur'an (see pages 9-11), is the law. The sexes are kept apart as much as possible, even in schools and colleges. Women cover themselves up almost completely when outside the home, as the Qur'an commands that they should only uncover themselves before their husbands or young children. In shops and offices, business stops whenever it is time to pray.

THE QUR'AN

When Muhammad preached Islam he spoke in rhyming prose (almost poetry). His teachings were so beautiful that many people believed they could only have come from God. This convinced them that they should become Muslims.

The Qur'an is written in various scripts, one of which is the *Maghrebi* script from North Africa.

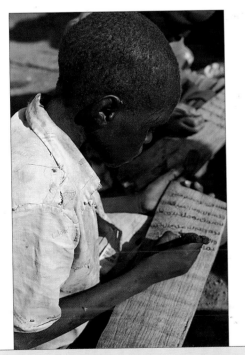

This Sudanese boy is learning to write out passages from the Qur'an.

During Muhammad's lifetime, the words of the Qur'an, the sacred book of Islam, were collected together. Qur'an is Arabic for 'recitation'. The Qur'an records the words God spoke through the Angel Gabriel to Muhammad to teach people about what they should believe and how they should live. Muslims believe that the Qu'ran records God's actual words. Many copies of the book were made and sent to different parts of the Muslim world.

THE QUR'AN TODAY

Every Muslim family treats its Qur'an with great care and respect. It is usually kept wrapped up in a fine cloth and placed on a high shelf, with nothing on top of it. It should only be touched with clean hands. When it is read it is placed on a rest so that it never touches the ground.

Modern Qur'ans. The making of beautiful books is a living tradition.

Most Muslims read the whole Qur'an and also learn passages from it as part of their education. Because they believe the Qur'an to be God's actual words, and therefore perfect, Muslims try to learn at least part of it in the original Arabic. Many Muslims can recite all the 114 chapters by memory. Someone who has learnt the whole Qur'an by heart is known as a *hafiz*.

Some of the most basic rules about Muslim life are laid down in the Qur'an. These cover what to eat and drink, as well as matters of family life, such as marriage, divorce and the care of elderly relatives. There is also extra guidance given in the *Hadith*. These are Muhammad's sayings and deeds explaining how to live out the words of the Qur'an in everyday life.

A Qur'an class in a Pakistani village, where Arabic is not the native language.

SPOTLIGHT

Some famous Hadith:
- 'He is not a true Muslim who eats as much as he wants while his neighbour goes hungry.'

- 'Someone who helps a widow or a poor person is like a warrior fighting for God.'

BEAUTIFUL BOOKS

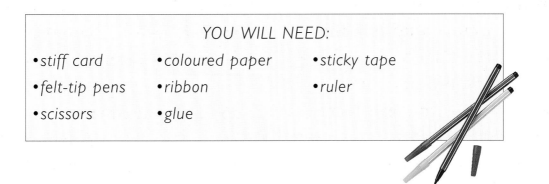

YOU WILL NEED:

- *stiff card*
- *felt-tip pens*
- *scissors*
- *coloured paper*
- *ribbon*
- *glue*
- *sticky tape*
- *ruler*

WHAT TO DO:

1 Lay your chosen book on the card and draw round it, leaving an extra 2cm to the left and right. Cut along your pencil lines.

3 Cut out and stick on paper shapes or use felt tips to decorate your book cover.

2 Place this card rectangle on coloured paper and draw cutting lines roughly 2cm outside the card shape. Cut out and glue onto the card.

4 Attach your cover to your book with coloured ribbon.

PRAYER

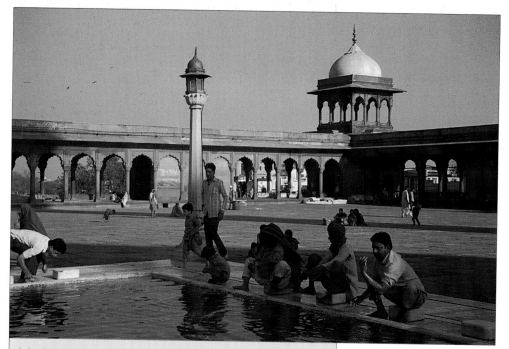

Muslims washing before prayer at the Friday Mosque, Delhi, India, one of the largest mosques in Asia.

DAILY PRAYERS

Muslims are supposed to pray five times a day, facing towards the Ka'ba in the holy city of Mecca, wherever they are in the world. The first prayer is said at dawn before sunrise. Other prayers are said at early afternoon, late afternoon, after sunset, and nightfall.

HOW TO PRAY

Before praying, Muslims must wash their hands, arms, feet and face. This washing is called *wudu*. As they pray, Muslims kneel and bow to show that they are humble before God. The prayers include parts of the Qur'an and are said in Arabic, even if it is not the person's own language. In these prayers, Muslims praise and thank God and ask for forgiveness and favour. Muslims are also allowed to add personal prayers asking for God's help. These prayers can be said in their own language.

WHERE TO PRAY

Prayers can be said anywhere so long as it is clean and, preferably, quiet. On Fridays, Muslims try to go to a mosque for the mid-day prayer. In many Muslim countries, Friday is a holiday with perhaps a few shops open in the early morning and evening. The prayers of the congregation are led by an *imam*. He is an expert on the Qur'an and the rules of Islam. Usually on Friday the imam preaches a sermon, explaining what Islam teaches about a current problem or event.

In most Muslim countries women can also go to the mosque, though many prefer to pray at home. In the mosque women sit separately from men, either at the back or upstairs in a gallery.

Muslims living in a non-Muslim country sometimes have problems keeping strictly to the requirements of their religion. For example, Muslims who work on a factory production line might find it impossible to leave their work to pray, or they may be unable to find a clean, quiet place for prayer. However, many Muslims still try to go to the mosque on Fridays.

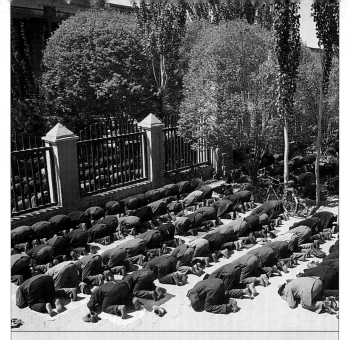

Chinese Muslims prostrate themselves in prayer. This shows a believer's submission to Allah (God).

Prayers can be said anywhere clean and, preferably, quiet.

MOSQUES

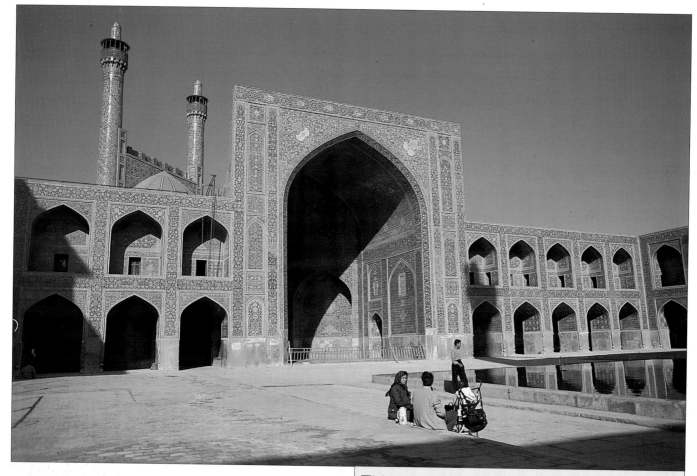

This mosque in Isfahan, Iran, is decorated with stunning tile-work. Classes were held in the alcoves.

The Muslim place of worship is a mosque, which means 'a place to bow down'. In many Muslim towns and villages, mosques are the largest and most beautiful buildings. Some of the most famous mosques are in Cairo in Egypt, Istanbul in Turkey and Isfahan in Iran.

MINARET AND MUEZZIN

Mosques are often used as schools and places for meetings or celebrations, as well as for worship.

Some mosques have a tall tower, called a minaret. In Muslim countries, this is where the call to prayer comes from. Traditionally, a man known as a *muezzin* stood at the top of the tower to deliver this call, five times a day. Now loud-speakers are used as the muezzin calls the people to prayer from inside the mosque, rather than from the minaret. Larger and more important mosques often have a dome. This represents the arch of the heavens

Mosques are all shapes and styles. This mosque in Mali, West Africa, is made of mud brick.

above the Earth, and reminds believers of God's power in making the whole universe.

COURTYARD AND CARPETS
Mosques usually have a large courtyard leading to a covered prayer-hall. There is a fountain or taps where worshippers can wash before praying. Shoes are left outside the prayer-hall to keep it clean.

Inside the prayer-hall there are no seats, but the floor of the prayer-hall is usually covered with carpets. The walls are often decorated with colourful patterns, or with writing

from the Qur'an. There are no pictures or statues inside the mosque because Muhammad banned them as aids to the worship of idols.

On one wall of the mosque is an alcove called a mihrab. This shows the direction of the Ka'ba in Mecca, so that people know the right way to face when they pray. Next to this alcove there is often a kind of pulpit, called a mimbar, from which the imam preaches his sermon, especially on Fridays.

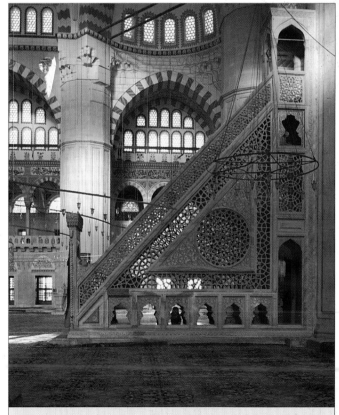

A marble mimbar (pulpit) at the Selimye Mosque, Edirne, Turkey.

MAKING A MOSQUE

YOU WILL NEED:

- shoe-box
- cardboard roll
- glue and sticky tape
- modelling clay
- paints and brush
- plastic lid
- lemon squeezer
- scissors
- aluminium foil
- drinking straws

WHAT TO DO:

1 Paint the inside and outside of a shoe-box to look like brick or pale stone. Leave it to dry.

2 Cut the lid into two unequal pieces. Use the shorter piece as the roof of the prayer hall. Paint it to match the rest of the box.

3 Cut the end flap off the remaining part of the lid and glue to the painted roof. Cut drinking straws to make supporting columns and stick inside with tape.

4 Glue the whole roof in place by squeezing it inside the box.

5 To make the dome, cover a lemon squeezer with a layer of modelling clay. When it is dry, take it off the lemon squeezer and paint it or cover it with aluminium foil. Glue it onto the roof, over the centre of the prayer hall.

6 To make the minaret, take the cardboard roll and paint it to match the rest of the mosque. Use the bottom section of a paper or polystyrene cup to make the balcony.

7 Now finish the mosque by making a small dome for the minaret. Use the lemon squeezer again but only cover the top part with clay. Again, leave to dry and paint when ready. Glue the whole minaret column in place. Make a washing pool by covering a plastic lid with aluminium foil. Decorate the mosque as you like, with flower or star patterns.

THE FIRST MUEZZIN

There was once a slave, called Bilal, who had a rich and cruel master, named Umayya. When Umayya found out that Bilal had become a Muslim, he tried to force him to go back to worshipping idols.

Umayya tortured Bilal in the desert outside Mecca. He forced him to lie down on the burning sand and placed a huge rock on his chest, so that he could hardly breathe. Then Umayya would say to Bilal, "Give up Islam! Or we'll go on like this until you die!"

As the days passed, Bilal grew weaker but his faith remained strong. However, even though he felt close to death, he still croaked out, "One God, One God..." when Umayya ordered him to give up Islam. Umayya laughed viciously. Bilal was famous for his lovely voice and now he could barely whisper.

One day, a wealthy man named Abu Bakr was walking in the desert and found Bilal in his weak state. Abu Bakr had first taught Bilal about Islam. He turned angrily to Umayya and asked him, "How can you be so cruel? Aren't you afraid of God's anger?"

Umayya replied with a snarl, "I won't be defied by a slave! And, anyway, you're the one to blame for teaching him your religion."

Abu Bakr looked at him calmly now and said, "Very well. If I caused your problem, I will solve it. Sell Bilal to me." "Glad to and good riddance," snapped Umayya and snatched some gold from Abu Bakr.

Abu Bakr helped Bilal back to Mecca, where he told him that he was no longer a slave. Bilal was now free to follow Islam as he wished. When Muhammad left Mecca for Medina, Bilal went with him.

When they arrived in Medina the Muslims built a mosque in which to pray. Now, Medina was not a city like Mecca but an oasis with houses scattered here and there. How could the people be summoned to pray at the mosque? There were plenty of ideas but none of them seemed right to everyone.

Then, one night, one of the Muslims dreamed that he was being called to prayer by a man's voice. Next day he told Muhammad about his dream.

"I believe God has sent us the answer to our problem," declared the Prophet. But who should do the calling? Many people wanted this honour.

Muhammad knew at once who would be the best - Bilal. Bilal was amazed to be chosen, then delighted, then confused. "I don't know what to say," he said.

"Say only what needs to be said," replied Muhammad.

So Bilal climbed up on to the roof of a house next to the mosque, cupped his hands around his mouth and boomed out the call to prayer. His rich, deep voice soared over the oasis and the words came out just right:

"*Allahu Akbar* - God is most Great. I declare that there is no god but God. I declare that Muhammad is the messenger of God. Come to prayer. Come to good work."

And so the slave, Bilal, became the first muezzin in the history of Islam.

Air travel means that people of all ages and many countries can travel to Mecca.

PILGRIM DRESS

When the pilgrims are about ten kilometres outside the city they must wash and change out of their ordinary clothes. Men put on two lengths of unsewn, white cloth. Women usually wear a long robe over their normal clothes. In these unadorned clothes, rich and poor all look alike in the sight of God. Many pilgrims save their pilgrimage garments to be buried in.

Once in a lifetime every Muslim should go on a pilgrimage to Mecca in Arabia, as the Qur'an commands them to if they can. Many then go on to Medina to visit the tombs of Muhammad and other early leaders of Islam. But Muslims should only go on pilgrimage if they are fit and their going does not cause hardship for their families.

The pilgrimage to Mecca is called the *Hajj*. Everyone who completes it can add the word *Hajji* to their name. Over two million pilgrims go to Mecca each year during *Dhu'l Hijja*, the twelfth month in the Muslim calendar, which is the month of pilgrimage.

The pilgrims' route from Mecca.

Pilgrims surround the Ka'ba at the heart of Mecca, Saudi Arabia

CEREMONIES AT SACRED PLACES

When they arrive in Mecca itself, the pilgrims walk seven times anti-clockwise around the sacred house known as the Ka'ba. Muslims believe that the Ka'ba was built by the prophet Abraham, and that Muhammad's grandfather was its guardian.

Then the pilgrims run seven times between the two low hills of Safa and Marwah. This recalls how Hagar, the ancestor of the Arab people, ran about the desert, looking for water for her son, Ishmael.

The pilgrims go to the Plain of Arafat. There, the pilgrims stand for

For one day in the year, the Plain of Arafat is a tented city of two million people.

a whole afternoon in the hot sun, praying and begging forgiveness for their sins. Muslims believe that it was here Adam and Eve had their sins forgiven by God.

STONING AND SACRIFICE

After spending the afternoon at Arafat, the pilgrims go to Muzdalifah to camp overnight and to gather pebbles. The next day, the pilgrims go to the village of Mina where they throw the pebbles at three stone pillars as a symbol of Abraham's rejection of the Devil. At Mina an

Pilgrims collecting stones at Muzdalifah, to throw at the pillars.

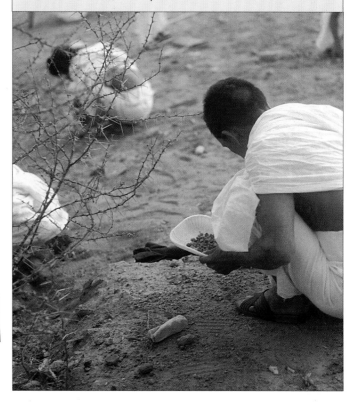

INTERVIEW

Some of my friends from college thought we were mad spending our money on a pilgrimage before we had paid for our house and car. But Allah doesn't tell us we have to have a house and a car. He tells us to go to Mecca if we can afford it.

Soleiman Abdullah, aged 32, Kuala Lumpur, Malaysia.

animal is sacrificed as an offering to God, and the meat is given away to the poor. Most pilgrims pay a professional butcher to do this. Then men have their heads shaved and women cut off at least 2.5 centimetres of their hair.

At the end of their pilgrimage, the pilgrims go around the Ka'ba another seven times. Many then go

Pilgrims touch the Ka'ba one last time before their journey home.

on to the city of Medina to visit the mosque of the prophet Muhammad. The pilgrims return home with many souvenirs of their visit, such as Zam-zam (holy water), prayer beads or prayer-carpets to give to their families and friends.

Shaving the head is a symbol of giving up personal vanity on the pilgrimage.

SPOTLIGHT

The Ka'ba is a cube-like building which now stands at the heart of Mecca's main mosque. Muslims believe that it was originally built by Adam, then later rebuilt by Abraham and his son Ishmael. As they were working on it, they were given a black stone by the Angel Gabriel which they built into one corner. Pilgrims try to touch or kiss the black stone as they walk round the Ka'ba.

FEASTING AND FASTING

Meal times are important as a way of gathering the whole family together, particularly at the end of Ramadan.

THE FAST OF RAMADAN

The ninth month of the Muslim calendar is called *Ramadan*. This is when Muhammad first began to hear revelations (messages) from God. Muslims remember this important event by fasting through the hours of daylight. This means not eating or drinking anything - to fast properly a person should not even take a sip of water. This is very hard to do in hot countries, where many Muslims live. In non-Muslim countries, keeping to a fast can be even harder. For example, Muslim children at school in non-Muslim countries might find it difficult to fast when friends all around them are eating snacks and lunches.

Muslims break their fast after sunset, when the whole family gathers to eat. Another meal is eaten just before dawn. Pregnant women, young children and very old people do not fast, nor do people who are ill.

FEASTING AT FESTIVALS

Two great festivals - *Eid al-Fitr* and *Eid al-Adha* - are celebrated by feasting, visiting relatives and giving presents. Eid al-Fitr means 'Festival of Fast-breaking', and it comes at the end of the month of Ramadan. Eid al-Adha means 'Festival of Sacrifice'. It is celebrated at the time when Muslims go on pilgrimage to Mecca (see pages 20-23).

Prayers to mark the end of Ramadan in Cameroon, West Africa.

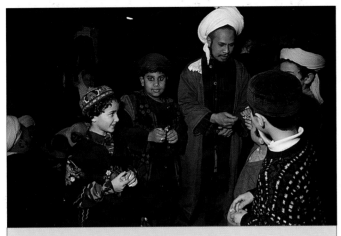
London children being given sweets to celebrate Eid al-Fitr.

HALAL AND HARAM

Muslims live in many different countries around the world, so they eat many different kinds of food. But all Muslims are forbidden by the Qur'an to eat certain things. Foods that are forbidden by the Qur'an are called *haram* (banned). Foods that are permitted and have been properly prepared are *halal* (lawful).

Haram items include anything made from a pig; meat with blood still in it; meat or fat from an animal that has not been killed correctly; and meat from a flesh-eating animal or an animal sacrificed to idols. Pig products include not only pork, ham and bacon but many other foodstuffs which contain pork fat, such as biscuits, ice-cream and soups.

Muslims are also forbidden to drink alcoholic drinks such as beer, wine or whisky.

For an animal's meat to be halal it must be killed by having the main vein in its neck cut with a sharp knife while the butcher pronounces the name of God. This is to show that the life of one of God's creatures is not being taken thoughtlessly.

In a real emergency, if no other food can be found, Muslims are allowed to eat even foods which are haram rather than starve to death.

INTERVIEW

I began trying to fast when I was about seven. Because we all have a big meal just before it gets light, it isn't so bad going without food. The hardest part is not drinking at all. When I came here from Morocco I thought it would be easier because it wasn't so hot. But here most people aren't Muslims, so there are cooking smells and people eating all around you.

Muhammad El-Baja, aged 13 London, UK.

MAKING A FRUIT DRINK

Many Muslims live in hot countries where iced fruit or yogurt drinks are very refreshing, particularly during the month of fasting.

YOU WILL NEED

- 5 oranges
- ice cubes
- sharp knife
- 1/2 tablespoon sugar (optional)
- glasses
- sieve
- saucepan
- lemon squeezer
- jug

WHAT TO DO:

1 Carefully cut the oranges in half and squeeze the juice out of them

3 (Miss out this stage if you don't want to add sugar.) Add the sugar and heat the orange juice and sugar in a saucepan until the sugar has dissolved.

2 Sieve the pips and flesh from the juice.

4 Serve with lots of ice and enjoy the drink with a friend.

The Muslim Family

A family enjoying themselves on a beach in Kuwait. The Muslim woman's main role is to bring up a happy family.

The family lies at the heart of Islam. The Qur'an gives special attention to the care of widows and orphans, whose families have been broken up by death.

The health and happiness of a family depends mainly on the mother. Her work in the home is considered to be just as important as the father's job. His main tasks are to provide the family with income and protection. Both parents have a duty to teach their children about Islam. Children should be learning to pray and fast by the time they are seven years old. Muslim children are expected to show respect to their parents and to look after them when they get old.

CUSTOMS AND CEREMONIES

The customs affecting birth, marriage and death vary in different parts of the Muslim world. But basic rules are widely accepted.

BIRTH

A child is regarded as a gift from God, and Muslims think a large family is a great blessing. The first words a baby hears are about God - '*Allah is the only God and Muhammad is his true Messenger*'. About seven days after birth, the baby is named and its head is shaved. The name often comes from a person famous in the history of Islam. All Muslim boys are circumcised. A Muslim doctor performs a simple operation to cut

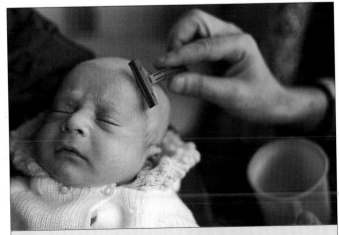

Muslim babies are named at a special ceremony, where their hair is also shaved.

the foreskin off the boy's penis. This may be done a few days after birth, or years later.

MARRIAGE

Marriage is seen as the joining together of two families, not just two people. Therefore parents often guide their children as to whom they will marry. However, they do not force their children to accept their choice. Muslims believe that love often becomes stronger when it grows out of an arranged marriage, rather than coming before it.

The simple wedding ceremony is made up of readings from the Qur'an and prayers. It is often led by

Different styles of dress at a Muslim wedding in Turkey.

an imam, but does not have to be as long as there are two adult male witnesses. The bride, groom and guests often wear splendid clothes and jewellery, give gifts and celebrate with a sumptuous meal. In some countries, a procession carries the bride from her parents' home to the home of her new husband. Divorce is permitted but is 'the most hateful of all permitted things'.

INTERVIEW

Most people don't understand about arranged marriages. It isn't just your own feelings you have to think about when you marry. You have to think of your family. When you are young you don't always know what is best for you. But your parents love you and want you to be happy. It would be un-Islamic to try and force you to marry someone. You could say that in Western countries people fall in love and then get married but in Muslim countries people marry and then fall in love.

Dr. Ayesha Riazz, aged 45, Lahore, Pakistan.

DEATH AND BURIAL

Muslims believe that after death they will be judged by God on the Day of Judgement when history comes to an end. Each person will be sent to heaven or hell according to how they lived their life.

When someone dies, their family washes the body for burial. Burial should follow as quickly as possible after death. Cremation (burning the body) is forbidden since the dead will have their bodies restored to life at the Day of Judgement and it is seen as a desecration of the body. Funerals should be simple and dignified. The body is buried with the face turned towards Mecca. Rather than spend money on an expensive gravestone, Muslims give the money to the poor.

The tombs of the faithful are aligned with Mecca at this cemetery in Tunisia.

When Prophet Muhammad met people who refused to believe in God, he would point to the sky and ask them who they thought had made the stars and planets. The regular movements of these heavenly bodies in the sky have often been taken as proof that the whole Universe follows an order set down by God. Patterns based on the constellations are often used to decorate mosques and Islamic works of art.

ASTRONOMY

Throughout history, Muslim scholars have taken a great interest in astronomy, the study of the stars and planets. Many stars have Arabic names such as Aldebaran ('the following'), or Algol ('the destruction'). In the past, astronomy had many practical uses. It allowed sailors to find their way across the oceans when they were out of sight of land. Travellers in the great deserts, where there were no reliable landmarks, could also steer by the stars to avoid getting hopelessly lost. The study of the stars and planets was also essential for making an accurate calendar and fixing the correct direction of prayer.

THE MUSLIM CALENDAR

The Muslim calendar is based on the movements of the Moon rather than the Sun. This means that the Muslim year is eleven days shorter than the year according to the calendar used in Western countries. The Western calendar begins with the birth of Jesus and is moving towards the 21st century. The Muslim calendar began when Muhammad moved from Mecca to Medina. It is now in its 15th century.

An 18th century observatory in India. Many stars have Arabic names.

DECORATED PLATES

WHAT TO DO:

1 Take your pencil and mark out two sets of lines, as shown here.

2 Join the lines together in whichever way you want to produce a star. Experiment to produce different types of stars. Mark out how many different areas you want to colour in.

3 Colour in your pattern to make a decorative plate. Patterns like this are used in Islamic art on mosques and other buildings. Sometimes these star patterns are very complicated.

GLOSSARY

Allah Arabic for God.

Congregation group of worshippers gathered for prayer.

Constellations groups of stars.

Cremation burning a dead body to reduce it to ashes.

Fasting going without food or drink as an act of religious discipline.

Hadith a record of traditional sayings about what the Prophet Muhammad said, did, or approved of.

Hafiz a person who has memorised all of the Qur'an.

Hajj pilgrimage to Mecca.

Halal something permitted by Islamic law.

Idol a man-made figure, usually of stone, wood, or metal, worshipped in the mistaken belief that it is holy.

Imam leader of Muslim congregation at prayer.

Islam the religion of Muslims; Islam means submitting to the will of God.

Judaism the Jewish religion.

Mihrab niche in a mosque wall showing the direction of prayer towards Mecca.

Minaret tower attached to a mosque, from which Muslims are often called to prayer by a muezzin.

Mimbar pulpit with stairs from which a sermon is preached at the Friday mid-day prayer.

Mosque building for the worship of Allah, also often used for meetings and teaching.

Muezzin official who calls Muslims to prayer.

Muslim a follower of Islam.

Oasis a well-watered, fertile patch of land in a desert region.

Orphaned losing one's parents.

Pagan a believer in idols or false gods.

Pilgrimage journey to a holy place.

Prophet a teacher with a message from God.

Prostrate to bow as low as possible as a sign of being humble before God.

Recitation saying something out loud.

Revelation a message from God.

Shrine a place for worship, often associated with a particular person.

Superstition a false belief.

Tomb burial plce.

Wudu act of washing before prayer.

INDEX